Looking at...
GANGS

Julie Johnson

WAYLAND

First published in 2009 by Wayland

Copyright © Wayland 2009

Wayland
338 Euston Road
London NW1 3BH

Wayland Australia
Level 17/207 Kent Street
Sydney NSW 2000

Produced for Wayland by
White-Thomson Publishing Ltd

+44 (0) 845 362 8240
www.wtpub.co.uk

Editors: Sonya Newland and Katie Powell
Designer: Robert Walster

British Library Cataloguing in Publication Data
Johnson, Julie
  Looking at gangs
  1. Gangs - Juvenile literature
  I. Title II. Gangs
  302.3'4

ISBN: 9780750259026

Picture Credits
AFP: 29; Associated Press: 6 (Tribune Star), 8, 13
(Macau Jornar Va Kio), 25 (Springfield Union News), 43;
Camera Press: 11 (Adrian Sutton); Chapel Studios: *title
page*, 5 (Tim Garrod); Corbis: 15 (China Newsphoto/
Reuters), 34 (Gideon Mendel); Dreamstime: 4 (Franz
Pflueg), 31 (Goodnewshoes), 32 (Goodnewshoes), 33
(Godfer); Angela Hampton Family Picture Library: 35, 36,
38, 39, 41, 45; Hodder Wayland Picture Library: *contents*
right (Tizzie Knowles), 18 (Chris Schwarz), 27 (Tizzie
Knowles), 30 (Martyn Chillmaid), 37 (Martyn Chillmaid),
40 (Chris Fairclough); iStock: *cover* (Rosemarie Gearhart
and Renee Lee); Pictorial Press: *contents* bottom, 13, 16,
20 (Jeffrey Mayer); Panos: 9 (Philip Wolmuth);
Popperfoto: 42; Popperfoto/ Reuters: 14, 17, 22, 23, 26,
28, 44; Tony Stone: 7 (David Young-Wolff); Unicorn: 10,
19, 21, 24.

Printed in China

Wayland is a division of Hachette Children's Books,
an Hachette UK company.
www.hachette.co.uk

Every attempt has been made to clear copyright.
Should there be any inadvertent omission please
apply to the publisher for rectification.

CONTENTS

What is a gang?

When you think of a gang, what picture comes into your mind? The group of friends you hang out with or a crowd of thugs? The dictionary says that a gang is a group of people who get together, sometimes to behave in an anti-social way. Gangs can be small or they can involve many people.

A gang is:
'A group of people who go round together and have a good time.'

'A group of people who are sometimes mean to other people.'
THOUGHTS FROM TWO NINE-YEAR-OLDS

'A group of people who cause trouble.'

'A group of people who look out for each other.'
THOUGHTS FROM TWO 15-YEAR-OLDS

← Most gangs are made up of young men, but there are some mixed and all-girl gangs, too.

A sense of belonging

You might have a 'gang of friends', but being part of a real gang is a bit different from just hanging out with friends. Gang members often give their gang a name. They might all wear the same clothes or develop a special language that only they can understand. This gives them a stronger sense of being part of a group.

Types of gangs

Some of the most serious crimes are carried out by gangs, but a gang can also be a group of people going along to watch their favourite football team. In this book, we will look mainly at gangs who bully others and commit crimes.

➡ The Bamboo Tribe is a Japanese gang. Its members are all fans of rock music, and they all wear leather bikers' jackets.

Rites and rituals

If someone wants to join a gang, they are often made to do things to prove they are 'worthy' of belonging. These are called initiation rites or rituals. For example, someone might have to promise to be loyal to the rest of the gang, and then prove their loyalty in some way.

⬆ The Ku Klux Klan is a racist organization in the USA. Klan members, dress in white and hold rituals in which they salute a burning cross.

Fun or frightening?

These rites can be harmless fun, but they can also be dangerous and frightening. If someone wants to join a street gang, for example, they might be beaten up to test how tough they are.

Tests of loyalty

Some gangs ask their members to do things that are dangerous, violent or against the law. They might make a new member hurt someone from another gang. They might dare the new member to run across a busy road or steal something from a shop. These are ways of testing how loyal the person will be to the gang in future.

➡ Daring a new gang member to steal goods from a shop is a way of testing her loyalty.

CASE STUDY ▸ CASE STUDY ▸ CASE STUDY ▸ CASE STUDY ▸

Paulo's gang has several different rituals that all new gang members have to go through before they can be accepted. First, they have to cross a railway line when a train is coming. This is to show how brave they are and to prove that the gang is important to them. To prove their strength and ability to stand up for themselves, they have to pick a fight with a boy in the gang or from another gang – and win.

Gang identity

Street gangs usually have particular ways of identifying themselves and marking their territory. Each gang has special hand signs that identify its own members. Fights between gangs may start when members of different gangs flash their hand signals at each other.

'We like to wear clothes with the Los Angeles Raiders' logo on them because it tells other gangs that we are tough and not to be messed with.'
DANNY, 15

Dress codes

The members of a gang might all wear clothes of the same colour, or they might all wear a similar item of clothing or jewellery. This could be a hat worn in a certain way, or a pendant or ring in a particular shape. Gang members might even have the same haircut. A gang member who chooses not to wear the 'uniform' of the gang risks getting beaten up.

➡ Members of Neo-Nazi gangs often have 'skinhead' haircuts, which make them look tough.

Body art

Members of street gangs often have tattoos
to show that they belong to a particular gang.
Some tattoos have special meanings – for
example, in many gangs, a spider's web
shows that a member has been in prison.

Street art

In areas where gangs hang out, walls
and buildings are often covered in graffiti.
Gangs use graffiti as a way of marking out
their territory. It might also be used to send
messages, challenge
other gangs or perhaps
to remember a gang
member who has
been killed.

➡ The hand signs these
men are making show that
they are members of the
Diamond Street gang in
Los Angeles, USA.

Street gangs

In many towns and cities around the world, there are young people who belong to street gangs. Research carried out in the USA shows that street gangs often form in cities where there are a lot of young people.

'They are dying to die...'
AN AMERICAN PRIEST, SPEAKING ABOUT GANG MEMBERS IN LOS ANGELES, USA

Living in fear

Street gangs are often involved in crime, especially stealing and drug-dealing. People who live in an area where there is a powerful gang may be afraid to report them to the police.

⬇ Members of the Tiny Locos gang show off their many tattoos.

American gangs

In the USA, there are four main gangs – the Crips and the Bloods in LA, and the Folk Nation and the People Nation, based in Chicago.

Russian gangs

In Russia, there are two main street gangs – the Neo-Nazi Skins and the Rappers, who are similar to the gangs that love rap music in the USA. Just off Red Square, in the middle of Moscow, these two gangs of young Russians often go head to head.

⬆ These masked men are members of the Crips gang.

'I will fight for my entire life for the right to wear trousers that hang down to my knees. We live only for ourselves. We devote all our time to break-dancing, graffiti and rap music.'
DENIS, A 17-YEAR-OLD RUSSIAN RAPPER

FACT

About 3,000 violent street gangs, motorcycle gangs and prison gangs with approximately 800,000 members operate in the US today.
FEDERAL BUREAU OF INVESTIGATION.

Criminal gangs

Some of the biggest criminal gangs are the Mafia in the USA, the Cosa Nostra in Italy, the Yazuka in Japan, the Triads in Southeast Asia and the Yardies from the Caribbean.

The Triads

Triad gangs have names like Sung Lion and Four Seas. These gangs control a large network of criminals and they have a lot of power in places such as Shanghai and Taiwan in China.

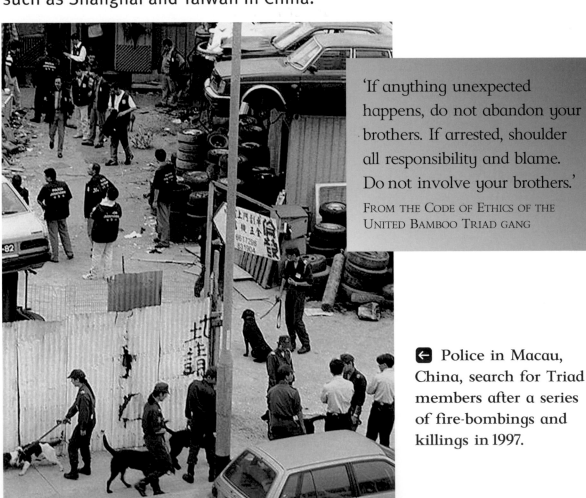

'If anything unexpected happens, do not abandon your brothers. If arrested, shoulder all responsibility and blame. Do not involve your brothers.'

FROM THE CODE OF ETHICS OF THE UNITED BAMBOO TRIAD GANG

← Police in Macau, China, search for Triad members after a series of fire-bombings and killings in 1997.

➡ A scene from *The Godfather*, a film all about the power of the Mafia in the USA.

The Yardies

Yardies are criminals who come from the poor part of Kingston, Jamaica. Today, groups of British-born young black men have begun to copy the Yardies, attracted by their 'glamorous' lifestyle. They drive expensive cars, deal drugs and commit crimes using automatic guns.

'The killings are worn as a badge of honour.'

A POLICE OFFICER WHO INVESTIGATED THE YARDIES' INVOLVEMENT IN VIOLENT CRIME

The Mafia

The Mafia is perhaps the most famous gang of all. Mafia gangs can be found in many countries, especially Italy and the USA. The series of films called *The Godfather* was about the Mafia. It showed how a big gang was organized, and how ruthless it could be with anyone who went against its interests.

The drugs trade

← These Colombian police officers are inspecting a sack of marijuana that they have discovered being secretly shipped to Italy.

Street gangs are often involved in drug-dealing, and a huge network of gangs controls the international trade in drugs. For example, a gang in the Far East might oversee the growing of plants that are used to make the drug heroin. The drugs are sold to bigger gangs that arrange for them to be smuggled to Europe and the USA.

Once there, smaller amounts of the drugs eventually reach local street gangs, which sell them in their area. Violence often breaks out as gangs struggle for a bigger share of the drugs trade.

FACT

42 per cent of youth gangs in the USA were involved in the street sale of drugs in order to make money for the gang.

NATIONAL YOUTH GANGS SURVEY.

The weapons trade

Drugs are not the only things that are traded illegally by gangs. Often, if the sale of something is restricted or forbidden, gangs move in. For example, if there is an international ban on selling weapons to a particular country, gangs may start illegally supplying that country with arms.

Protection rackets

Gangs such as the Triads also operate protection rackets. This is when a gang forces owners of local businesses to pay money in exchange for protection from other gangs. People who refuse to pay the gang, or who do not have enough money to pay, may be beaten up. Their shops or restaurants may be damaged.

⬇ These members of a Chinese mafia-like gang have been arrested for illegal activities.

Are gangs new?

Gangs have been around for centuries. Stories from ancient Greek and Roman times describe groups of young men attacking and beating up other young men. Shakespeare's play *Romeo and Juliet*, written in the 1590s, tells the story of two family gangs, the Capulets and the Montagues. A film version of this story shows them as modern gangs in New York.

The first American gangs

In nineteenth-century America, Irish immigrants began to form gangs. One, the Forty Thieves, had dress codes and a strong leader. The gang called its members by special coded nicknames.

← The Capulet gang prepares to take on the Montagues, in the film version of *Romeo and Juliet*.

FACT

In Los Angeles, 59 per cent of all murders are gang-related. In Chicago, 53 per cent are gang-related.

US DEPARTMENT OF JUSTICE, 2008.

Growing gangs

By the 1920s, there were 1,313 gangs in Chicago. By the 1940s, Mexican-American gangs ruled the streets of Los Angeles. The motorcycle gang Hell's Angels was formed in 1948 in California. The different groups of Hell's Angels are called 'chapters'. Today, there are more than 70 chapters in Europe, as well as chapters in Australia, New Zealand and South Africa.

⬇ These bikers are members of a South African chapter of the Hell's Angels gang.

Gangs with guns

The number of gangs in the USA has continued to grow. It is now easier than ever to buy guns, so gangs have become more violent. With more guns, and more gang members owning cars, the number of drive-by shootings has increased in the past few years.

Why do people join gangs?

FACT

Most youth gang members are between the ages of 12 and 24, and the average age is about 17 to 18 years.

NATIONAL YOUTH VIOLENCE PREVENTION RESOURCE CENTER.

Everyone wants to feel like they belong. Joining a gang can be a normal part of growing up. For some teenagers, their friends may become more important to them than their families. This is the age when young people are most likely to join a gang.

➡ For most young people, hanging out with friends is fun and harmless.

Family or friends?

For some teenagers, joining a gang is a way of rebelling against their family. Their parents may have broken up, or they may have grown up in foster care or in a children's home. Being in a gang makes these people feel secure.

Family ties

Sometimes young people are *expected* to join a gang. In Italy and the USA, Mafia gangs are often made up of several members of one family.

⬇ For some people, gangs can provide closer relationships than their own families.

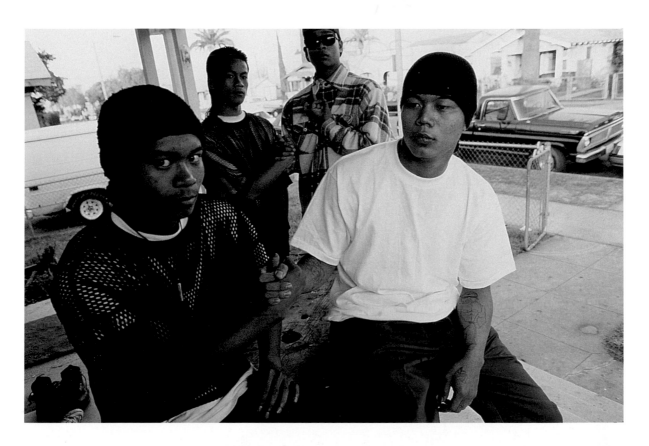

Joining street gangs

People join street gangs for many different reasons. Films and gangsta rap music can make gang life seem cool and glamorous. There may be pressure from friends to join a gang. Some people join so they are protected from other gangs.

'We had a gang on the estate where I grew up — we felt part of something and had fun together. Didn't really do anything wrong except knock on people's doors and run away.'
ELDERLY BRITISH MAN

← Gangsta rap star Snoop Dogg has been in trouble with the law, but he still has many fans.

Other reasons why people join street gangs are:

- They are poor and think that joining a gang is an easy way to make money.

- They are unemployed and being an active gang member is something to do.

- They are discriminated against: many people from ethnic minorities join gangs.

- They live in poor areas from which there seems no escape. Belonging to a gang can offer excitement and adventure.

⬆ Owning a big car can be a status symbol for many gang members.

FACT

100 per cent of cities with more than 250,000 people reported gang activity.

NATIONAL YOUTH GANG SURVEY.

Outsiders

In any school or neighbourhood there are usually a few people who are seen as different in some way. Often, these people are bullied or left out. They might get together with other people in the same situation and form their own gangs for protection. Gangs like this might fight back against the people who have bullied them.

⬇ Students at Columbine High School write messages on the coffin of one of the girls who was killed.

FACT

In 1999, Eric Harris and Dylan Klebold shot dead several students and teachers at Columbine High School in Colorado, USA, and then killed themselves. The two boys were members of a school gang, known as the Trenchcoat Mafia because of the coats they all wore. One of the other gang members told a news reporter that the gang had been teased by other students. This may have played a part in triggering the murders.

← Young Neo-Nazis marching in Germany. Neo-Nazi gangs have carried out attacks on immigrants.

Ethnic minorities

People who belong to an ethnic minority may feel unwelcome. By forming a gang with other members of their ethnic group, they might feel they are less likely to be attacked.

Some people join gangs because they feel their way of life is under threat. For example, gangs of racists may claim that their country is being 'swamped' by foreigners. The people who join these gangs may feel they have to compete with people from different cultures for a job.

The trouble with gangs...

When young people join gangs they may begin to do things that they would never do if they were on their own. They may start committing crimes or taking drugs, for example. This is called developing a 'gang mentality'.

Gang mentality

The first time a gang member steals a car or sprays graffiti on a wall, it seems really daring. The gang members encourage each other. They may get a buzz from doing something illegal. This good feeling makes them want to do it again – and next time it seems much easier.

➡ Graffiti-covered buildings are a common sight in gangland areas.

This man is a member of the Latin Kings street gang in Massachusetts, USA.

The buzz from bad behaviour

To keep getting a kick from their activities, gangs sometimes find they need to take bigger and bigger risks. They might begin by vandalizing cars, then move on to stealing car radios. Eventually they will steal cars and start joy-riding. They feel there is less chance that they will be identified if they are in a group.

Where does it end?

Sooner or later, these people get a reputation as troublemakers. If they are involved in dangerous activities they might be injured, or even killed. They might get involved with bigger gangs that commit serious crimes. Some will get caught by the police.

'I never thought I would end up in prison. It all started with nicking things from the local shop next to school when I was nine.'
GRAHAM, 20

Substance abuse

Sometimes gang members become involved in substance abuse. This might include sniffing glue or aerosol sprays, or using illegal drugs such as cannabis, cocaine or heroin. Drugs may be easily available in the poor areas where gangs often live. Many gangs deal in drugs as well as using them.

⬇ This homeless boy belongs to a street gang in Manila in the Philippines. He is sniffing glue.

Why take drugs?

At first, substance abuse can seem daring. The drug makes the user feel good, and taking risks can also be exciting. Someone might enjoy taking part in a secret activity that is shared only with other gang members.

CASE STUDY ▸ CASE STUDY ▸ CASE STUDY ▸ CASE STUDY ▸

'I was brought up on an estate where drugs were just part of life. Everyone was using them and when I joined the gang it just seemed the right thing to do. It all started with sniffing glue and then I got into cannabis. After that I got caught nicking some things from a local shop. I was planning to sell the stuff and use the money to buy cannabis. It just went on from there. I couldn't get out of the gang — I owed one of them money for drugs and he just kept making me nick more and more things.'

STEVE, 16

Gang addicts

It is not always easy to stop taking drugs once you have started. People can become addicted. Drug addicts often have to steal the money they need to buy more drugs. They are addicted to an activity they carry out as part of a gang, so they may find it very difficult to leave the gang, even if they want to.

➡ Drug users who cannot pay for the drugs they use may be beaten up.

Gangs and violence

Not all gangs are violent, but people often link gangs and violence. Gangs attract people who want to seem tough. They might challenge people in their own gang to a fight, or attack members of other gangs.

Why are people violent?

People can be violent for the same reason as they take drugs or steal cars – it gives them a buzz. They feel powerful because they are part of a gang. They may pick on particular people, such as those from a different ethnic group.

⬇ British teenager Stephen Lawrence was murdered by a racist gang. His parents complained that the police did not investigate the murder properly.

Turf wars

Street gangs sometimes become involved in 'turf wars' to protect their territory from rivals. Often gangs make a lot of money from activities like drug-dealing. If other gangs move in, the local gang may fight to protect its income.

← A police officer checks a suspected gang member for weapons.

FACT

In 2005, there were 1,746 gang-related murders in the USA.

NATIONAL YOUTH GANGS SURVEY.

CASE STUDY ▸ CASE STUDY ▸ CASE STUDY ▸ CASE STUDY ▸

Mario, 17, lives in an inner-city neighbourhood. One day, a gang from another neighbourhood showed up. They walked around as if they owned the place. The local boys felt angry. Eventually, they organized themselves into a gang. They wanted to protect their territory from the invaders. There was some fighting, but it stopped when some older boys brought both gangs together to sit down and talk about it. The other gang left. Mario and his friends did not have any more problems and have disbanded the gang, as they feel they do not need it any longer.

Bullying

Gangs can be found in all types of school. Children want to feel that other people like them, and joining a gang is a way of feeing accepted.

CASE STUDY ▸ CASE STUDY ▸

When 11-year-old Max started his new school, there was a group of boys who called themselves 'The Boys'. Everyone seemed to want to be part of this gang. Max had been bullied at his old school and his dad had told him to get in with the big boys to stop it happening again. Max really just wanted to make some friends. One of the gang members lived in the same street as him and he seemed friendly. Max decided to hang around with him, and eventually he got into the gang. No one picked on him when he was with the gang and his dad was really pleased. The only problem was that Max had no real friends outside the gang.

← Lonely people often want to join a gang so they can have friends.

School gangs

There are different types of school gang. Some are tough gangs – perhaps the biggest boys or girls in the school. They might have older brothers or sisters who belong to street gangs. Some are cool gangs, whose members know all about the latest music. Other gangs are gangs of bullies. Children outside the gang may be afraid of these groups – or they may wish that they were more like them.

⬇ Gangs of boys like this one can be intimidating for other children, even if they are just hanging out.

What is bullying?

Bullying is when one person or a group of people hurt someone else on purpose, either physically or mentally. School gangs often bully other children because being part of a gang makes people feel safer and more powerful.

'She doesn't touch me or hit me. It's just the way she looks at me and says "I'll get you". I think she will get me one day.'

LISA, 11

Types of bullying

Bullying can take many different forms. Some bullies may tease other children and make cruel comments. Others may hit them or physically hurt them in other ways.

⬇ Gangs of 'cool' kids may hang around outside school, waiting to intimidate other children.

Standing up to bullies

Some people still believe that bullying is harmless. They think that victims of bullying should just stand up for themselves.

But bullying can make people feel too afraid to stand up for themselves. Fighting back may get the victim into trouble. Some people have been bullied so much that they have committed suicide. Today, schools and parents realize how harmful bullying can be, and take the problem very seriously.

⬆ Gangs may tease and laugh at other children, or they may use physical violence against them.

'They push and shove me, or trip me up whenever we pass in school.'
Paul, 12

Why do people bully?

People join gangs of bullies for many different reasons. Some children find it difficult to get on with others. They may come from a home where their parents fight with each other. They may not have been taught how to work things out with other people.

Other children may have been spoilt at home. They may not be told off when they do things that are wrong. They might not have been taught to think about other people's feelings.

⬇ A teacher deals with bullying in the playground. Children can start bullying from a young age if they are not taught right from wrong at home.

CASE STUDY ▶ CASE STUDY ▶ CASE STUDY ▶ CASE STUDY ▶

Twelve-year-old Marsha knew things were not good between her mum and dad. They were always shouting at each other, her dad came home from work later and later, and then suddenly he just left. No one really talked to Marsha about what was going on. She was angry and confused.

Marsha joined a gang at school and started bullying other children. The school contacted her mother, who was angry with Marsha, saying she had enough to deal with already. Marsha felt that no one was considering her feelings. The bullying was just a way of letting out her anger.

➡ **Talking to your parents or an adult you trust may help if you are feeling angry or left out.**

Wanting attention

Some people bully because they have been bullied themselves. They think the best way to stop it is to bully others.

There may have been big changes at home that children are finding difficult to cope with. There may be a new baby, or their parents may have split up. They feel left out or angry. Bullying is a way of drawing attention to themselves.

Who gets bullied and why?

Some people are more likely to be bullied than others. Gangs often pick on people they see as different from themselves. Their victim might wear glasses or be overweight, or come from a different ethnic group or a poorer family than the gang members.

'I used to pick on other kids who were going through a hard time. It made me feel better about all the things going on at home for me.'

LISA, 14

← Bullies like Lisa will often target people who have problems at home or at school.

Easy victims

Gangs also bully children who already seem unhappy because they see them as easy targets. Children who do not feel good about themselves may even feel that they deserve the bullying.

⬆ Victims of bullying can find it hard to trust other children and make friends.

The effects of bullying

Some children find ways to deal with the bullying on their own and it stops. In these cases, it may not have done much harm. But others find it more difficult to handle.

'I shall remember this for all eternity. Monday: My money is taken. Tuesday: Names are called. Wednesday: My uniform is torn. Thursday: My body is pouring with blood. Friday: It's ended. Saturday: Freedom.'

AN ENTRY IN THE DIARY OF 13-YEAR-OLD VIJAY SINGH, WHO COMMITTED SUICIDE

Doing nothing

When a gang is bullying someone, other people often know what is going on. Why don't they do anything to stop it?

⬆ Children sometimes admire a gang for being tough, instead of trying to stop their behaviour.

Just watching...

Sometimes it is just easier to stand by and watch than to get involved. People may be afraid that if they try to stop the bullying, the gang will pick on them next. They might want to be accepted by the gang. Some people even enjoy watching someone else being bullied, even if they are not a bully themselves.

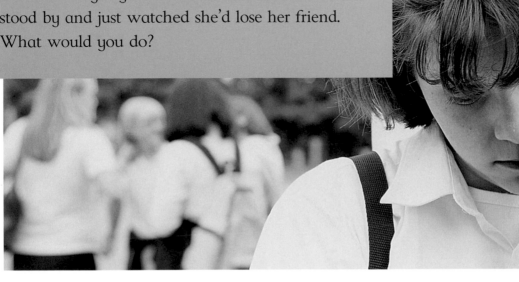

CASE STUDY ▸ CASE STUDY ▸

Katie had been bullied in her primary school and now just kept her head down. When her best friend started being bullied by Natalie's gang, she didn't know what to do. If she stood up to them she might get bullied as well. But if she stood by and just watched she'd lose her friend. What would you do?

Difficult choices

Doing nothing makes the bullies more powerful. It makes the gang feel that no one dares stand up to them. The victim feels even more alone.

There are several choices to make if you see bullying taking place. You could stand up to the gang. You could tell an adult what is going on. Or you could choose to walk away. Each of these options has a consequence. Remember, doing nothing gives power to the gang. Next time, the victim could be you.

⬆ People often push the problem of bullying to the back of their mind and hope it stops.

Dealing with bullying

When dealing with bullying it is important to remember the two T's: Telling and Talking.

Some children are afraid they will be called a 'snitch' or a 'grass' if they tell an adult about bullying, but it is okay to tell. Sometimes people feel the bullying will get worse if they tell. But if they don't tell, the gangs of bullies will carry on anyway, and they are probably picking on other people as well.

⬇ It takes courage to tell on a bully — victims often fear the problem will just get worse.

THAT LONG ROAD
Walking up that road to school
    I consider turning back,
I consider running to that special
    point, my own special point.
I consider going to their houses
    and telling their mums.
I consider ruining their lives
    somehow — to make them
    feel scared.
Then suddenly I'm in school, they
    take my bag, ruffle my hair.
Maybe some other day.
KATE

Help and counselling

Talking about what is happening can help people feel better. Many victims of bullying want to deal with it themselves. They often just need some ideas and support in order to handle the bullies. Talking to a school counsellor, teacher or parents can help. Friends can help, too.

Help to stop being a bully

Sometimes the bullies want to stop bullying but don't know how. If they belong to a gang they may be under pressure to keep bullying. A school counsellor could help find ways of breaking the bullying habit.

⬇ Telling a parent can be the first step to solving a bullying problem.

Leaving a gang

Most people only belong to a gang for a short period of time. There are as many different reasons for people leaving gangs as there are for them joining.

Gangs for ever?

Joining a gang can be a normal part of growing up. As people get older they usually feel more confident. They don't feel they need to belong to a gang any more. Some gang members decide to leave once they have children to care for. They may not want to take the risks involved with drugs or crime.

↓ As they grow older, many people find they get the 'buzz' they once got from gang activities from other things, such as sport.

FACT

Studies of gangs done since the 1920s have shown that most young people stay in a gang for no more than one year.

STUDIES BY MILLER AND SPERGEL.

↑ A Guardian Angel on patrol in Detroit, USA.

Life changes

Some people leave gangs when they move to a new area or change schools. They have a chance to make new friends and leave their old life behind. When people get a job they may find they no longer have time for the gang, or they find that their interests change.

FACT

The Guardian Angels were set up in New York in 1979 and are now found in many US cities. Guardian Angel groups are mostly made up of teenagers who have managed to break free from violent gangs. They patrol the streets, parks and underground stations, trying to keep ordinary people safe from gang violence.

Making the break

Some people find it easy to leave a gang, but for others it is much more difficult. Gang members who have promised to be loyal may find it hard to break that promise. Other gang members may put pressure on them to stay.

Leaving street gangs

'Jumping out' is when a gang member suddenly decides to leave a street gang. Other gang members feel betrayed and they make it very difficult for that person to leave. They will let people go, but not before they have beaten them up to teach them a lesson. These beatings are much worse than the ones given during an initiation rite.

⬇ This Mafia member in Sicily decided to give evidence about other gang members to the police. He needed close protection, in case the Mafia tried to kill him.

Fading out

An easier and safer way to leave a street gang is to 'fade out'. This means that you gradually stop hanging out with the gang. Eventually, you stop going out with them altogether.

⬆ Parents, teachers and counsellors can help in deciding how best to leave a gang.

Police protection

Gang members who have been involved in serious crime might ask the police for help in leaving a gang. They give the police information about the gang, and in return, the police will protect them. But for most young people, leaving a gang is not quite so dangerous. Talking to an adult and making new friends can be a good start.

GLOSSARY

Addiction

When a person cannot stop doing something, even when it is harmful.

Anti-social behaviour

Behaviour that makes life unpleasant for people around you, but is not actually illegal.

Automatic gun

A gun that keeps firing bullets automatically for as long as the trigger is pulled.

Break-dancing

A type of street dancing, usually to hip-hop music, involving jumps and turns, standing up and on the ground.

Chapter

Another word for gang, used to refer to groups of Hell's Angels.

Code of ethics

Rules that set out how gang members should behave.

Drive-by shooting

Shooting someone from a vehicle as it drives past.

Ethnic minorities

Groups whose language, skin colour, religion or traditions are different from most of the other people in a country.

Grafitti

Painting or writing on walls or public buildings. Some gangs use grafitti as a way of marking out their territory.

Heroin

A very addictive drug, made from morphine, that is usually injected by users.

Immigrants

People who have left one country to go and live in a different one.

Intimidate

To scare or threaten.

Joy-riding

Driving a stolen car, often in a dangerous way.

Ku Klux Klan

A racist organization in the USA that targets African Americans.

Mafia

A secret criminal organization that began in Sicily. The word 'mafia' is often used to mean any large criminal organization.

Neo-Nazis

People who have very extreme political views, including the idea that white people are better than other people.

Racists

People who hate people from other cultures.

Rap

Songs in which the words are chanted or spoken to a beat. Gangsta rap music is often about violence or urban street life.

Rites

A series of rituals that are carried out for a particular purpose, for example to mark someone's acceptance into a gang.

Ritual

An action that has to be carried out in a particular way, often as part of a ceremony.

Substance abuse

Using substances such as alcohol or glue in a way that can damage your health.

Suicide

Killing yourself.

Tattoos

Pictures and symbols on the body made by injecting ink under the skin.

Vandalism

Destroying or damaging public or private property.

FURTHER INFORMATION

ORGANIZATIONS

Anti-Bullying Campaign
185 Tower Bridge Road
London SE1 7UF
Tel: 020 7378 1446
www.bullying.co.uk

ChildLine
Tel: 0800 1111
www.childline.org.uk
A free confidential 24-hour helpline
for children and young people in
trouble or danger

The Drug Education Forum
c/o Mentor UK
4th Floor, 74 Great Eastern Street
London EC2A 3JG
Tel: 020 7739 8494
www.drugeducationforum.com

Institute for the Study of Drug
Dependence (Drugscope)
Prince Consort House
Suite 204 (2nd Floor)
109/111 Farringdon Road
London EC1R 3BW
Tel: 020 7520 7550
www.drugscope.org.uk

Home Office: Tackling Drugs,
Changing Lives
2 Marsham Street
London SW1P 4DF
Tel: 020 7035 4848
www.drugs.homeoffice.gov.uk

Release
388 Old Street
London EC1V 9LT
Tel: 020 7729 5255
www.release.org.uk

Re-Solv
30a High Street, Stone,
Staffs ST15 8AW
Tel: 01785 817885
Free helpline: 0808 800 2345
www.re-solv.org

Victim Support
Hallam House
56–60 Hallam Street
London W1W 6JL
Tel: 020 7268 0200
www.victimsupport.org.uk
Help and advice for victims of crime

FURTHER READING

Books for children
Talk About: Bullying
by Jane Bingham
(Wayland, 2008)

Talking About: Bullying
by Bruce Saunders
(Watts, 2007)

Fiction
Drive-by
by Lynne Ewing
(HarperCollins, 1998)

The Bathwater Gang
by Jerry Spinelli
(Little, Brown & Co, 2005)

The Chase
by Nancy N. Rue
(Focus on Family Publishing, 1999)

Looking at... Gangs

INDEX

48